KITTY CAT'S MOTOR IS RUNNING!

Bil Keane

FAWCETT GOLD MEDAL • NEW YORK

A Fawcett Gold Medal Book
Published by Ballantine Books
Copyright © 1981 by Register and Tribune Syndicate, Inc.
Copyright © 1985 by Cowles Syndicate, Inc.

Library of Congress Catalog Card Number: 85-90742

ISBN 0-449-12422-3

Manufactured in the United States of America

First Ballantine Books Edition: December 1985

10 9 8 7 6 5 4 3 2 1

"No wonder <u>Kittycat</u> acts so bored. We don't
have any <u>mouses</u> around here."

"I'm not allowed out and just because of something I didn't do — my homework."

"I think my eyes are gettin' ready to take a nap."

"Oooh! Kittycat's tongue is made of sandpaper!"

"I'm glad you met Mommy, 'cause I wouldn't
like not being here."

"And Joseph couldn't get them a room 'cause all the motels were overbooked."

"Lots of people let their kids draw the card
they send out, so I drew this picture of Santa
for our card. Do you like it?"

"I'm asking for that one, Dolly. You can ask for the next one."

"Is somebody babysitting the elves
while you're here?"

"The child is three and the father is not
mechanically inclined."

"Those aren't Christmas trees, Daddy.
They don't have lights."

"Grandma says she's not gonna bother putting
up a tree at her place this year 'cause nobody
ever comes to see it."

"I always know when it's Christmastime 'cause I can smell it."

"What I DON'T want is clothes."

"But I don't wanna just hand it to you, Daddy. I
wanna climb up and hang it myself."

"It's the best tree we've ever had!"
"Aw, Mommy, you say that every year."

"I have $1.25 left for daddy's present,
Mommy. Will you put in the rest?"

"Poor little baby Jesus—he only got, gold, frankincense and myrrh—no toys."

"... Holy instant so tender and mild. . . ."

"Don't you hafta go up on the roof to hang
them by the chimney with care?"

"EDITOR'S NOTE: Seven-year-old Billy helps Daddy out with this Christmas Day drawing."

"... And I got a race car and a ...."

"Santa can't see us any more—he's back at the
North Pole."

"Does Jack Frost belong to Santa Claus, Mother Goose or Disney?"

"I've written Aunt Nancy's, Grandma's and Aunt Peg's. We don't hafta write thank you notes to Santa, do we?"

"PJ pulled everything out of all those handbags on your bed."

"Huh? Oh, we were watchin' for the new year
to get here and I guess we fell asleep."

"Mommy! The snow grew last night!"

"You just wait! Wait till you grow up and have dolls of your own!"

"In the olden days kids pushed Hula-Hoops with sticks."

"We're all inside that little round thing and Daddy has to take it to the store to get us out."

"Mommy, tell Kittycat to turn off her claws!"

"The new teacher learned my name today. I knocked over her coffee."

"Look, Mommy! I have one bang."

"This slice has a knothole in it."

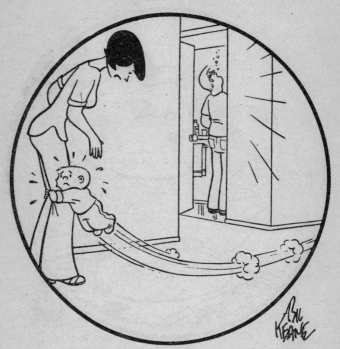

"That's just daddy gargling."

"Wanna hear a funny one? In sex ed today a
kid said his father thinks STORKS
bring babies."

"I could've made it look more like you but you moved."

"How come the <u>birds</u> aren't eating at our <u>feeder</u>?"

"We learned how to make an <u>A</u> in real <u>grown</u>-up writing."

"Will you empty these cans for dinner, Mommy? I need them for a project."

"Mommy! Daddy zipped up my coat and gave me an uppercut to the chin!"

"We weren't jumping on the bed. We were jumping OFF it."

"Bet I know what babies like about being born.
They can stretch."

"Snow is quiet and you can see it. Thunder is
noisy but you CAN'T see it."

"You can't sit there, P.J. That chair is preserved."

"Don't turn the page yet!"

"Can we use this basket, Mommy? We're playin' church."

"Why do they put baby powder on marshmallows?"

"You are never to eat with your hands."
"What about when we have sandwiches?"

"Your ruler <u>has</u> lots of <u>elbows</u>."

"Look, Daddy — LIGHTNING!"

" . . . and that's what <u>Marmaduke</u> is doing today. Next—<u>Heathcliff</u> the cat. . . ."

"Is it all right if I tell God to have a nice day?"

"Grandma put PJ's stringbeans on her plate
and NOW he likes them."

"I don't like this toothbrush. Its brustles are too hard."

"Father Forrest said people are made out of dust. Who are we putting together up here?"

"Dolly used my comb and left her tangles in it."

"NOTHING'S wrong. We were just seeing who
could sing highest."

"Billy said an X-rated word."

"Mommy, will you watch my building for me
today so PJ doesn't knock it down?"

"Would you be <u>mad</u> if I loved Miss Piggy best,
next to you?"

"That's very good, Mommy. But why are the
birds all flying upsidedown?"

"Mommy, is there any way to divorce brothers?"

"I was holding it for Mommy, not for
you, Dolly."

"I'll always love you, Mommy. And I'll always remember your name."

"I don't care for this cherry pie. I wish George Washington chopped down a blueberry bush."

"I feel just a LITTLE sick. Enough to stay home from school, but not enough to stay in bed."

"100? You mean I have a perfect temperature?"

"Billy's cake might get stale by the time he's
well enough to eat it, so can I have it?"

"This is the work Billy missed in school. His teacher said you could help him."

"Billy broke the bed's rib!"

"Hi, Daddy! Did you bring us some
little soaps?"

"You forgot to put a catastrophe in 'don't'."

"There's no fingernail on this shoelace."

"He always locks the gasoline in, but it keeps
getting out of there some way."

"I like the inside of an orange, but
not the crust."

"Don't worry, <u>Mommy</u>, we won't catch cold.
We're eating lots of <u>cough drops</u>."

"Will you load my toothbrush for me, Mommy?"

"Mommy put a new hat on my pencil."

"When **PJ** said that word last week you laughed and everybody thought it was cute."

"He hasn't been outside today because he has an upset stomach."

"Are you and Daddy OK for money?"

"I'm trying to practice my reading but Dolly won't listen."

"But I didn't ASK Grandma for a piece of her cake. It was her idea."

"Walls hold rooms together."

"I can't find <u>any</u> socks in my drawer that <u>look</u> the <u>same</u>."

"Mommy, how do you dial the hyphen?"

"The car threw up _and_ we hafta wait till it _gets_ better."

"Why are you throwing them away?"

"Don't cut my sandwich in quarters, Mommy.
The guys will think I'm a baby."

"I'm practicing to be a daddy."

"Jeffy's making ice cream soup."

"Can I use that crayon when you're finished with it?"

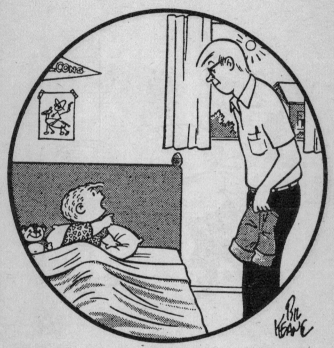

"Could you turn out the sun so I can take my nap?"

"I'll never understand grown-ups if I live to be eight."

"You better hold my hand, <u>Mommy</u>, so I don't fall off this <u>high</u> wall."

"This celery is good. Mommy put peanut butter in the ditch."

"The top part of this mirror doesn't get much wear 'cept when mommy and daddy are looking in it."

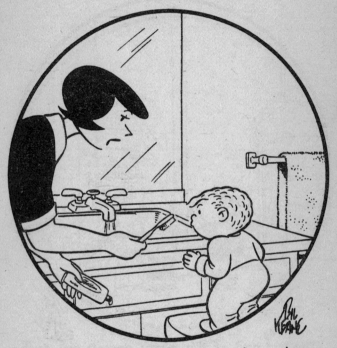

"It's the same as the electric one, only you have to wiggle it yourself."

"It's <u>PJ</u>'s favorite toy—the <u>TV</u> remote <u>control</u>."

" . . . and know what else, Grandma? Mommy
got real mad at Daddy 'cause he. . . ."

"That move doesn't count 'cause I didn't let go
of the checker yet."

"Mommy! Wake up! We missed the bus!"   "APRIL FOOL!"

"Why do tangerines have such baggy skins?"

"Mommy! It's coming out the wrong place!"

"I like the way Daddy fixes eggs — with brown
lace around the edges."

"It's raining, Mommy. We'll need our underbrella."

"Some of those raindrops are scoring two points."

"I'll have the same as Mommy — a hot roast beast sandwich."

"P.J. thinks he's dancing, but he's just bouncing up and down over and over again."

"I didn't know this street had a downstairs."

"Why is the man shaving our <u>window</u>?"

"Can we have some junk food?"

"We had the whole puzzle put together and PJ
tried to pick it up to show it to you."

"If I ever get to be an angel I'd rather play a guitar."

"Tattletale! Tattletale! Tattletale!"

"Mommy! Billy's callin' me a tattletale!"

"I've got eight yellow ones, seven green ones, three black ones, five purple ones . . . ."

"Did they have Easter yesterday in your town, too, Grandma?"

"Closer, Mommy. I can't read the bumper
sticker."

"We'll be by the <u>comic books</u>, Mommy . . . and
if we're not there we'll be by the <u>toys</u>,
and if we're not there we'll be
by the <u>candy</u>, and. . . ."

"That was fun! Open the door and let another
one in."

"Is a <u>triple</u> play when the guy trips over the <u>base</u>?"

"Birds are very useful. They eat <u>harmful</u> insects and <u>breadcrusts</u>."

"I guess it's a good thing cats can't laugh out loud."

You can have lots more fun
with
BIL KEANE and
THE FAMILY CIRCUS